ME AND MY SENSES

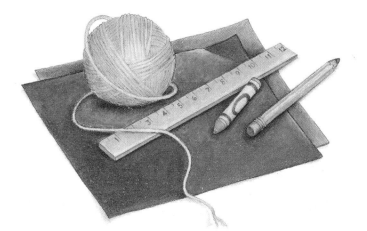

by Joan Sweeney   illustrated by Annette Cable

Crown Publishers ♛ New York

For our latest sensation, Liam
—J.S.

In memory of Mom
love, A.C.

Text copyright © 2003 by Joan Sweeney
Illustrations copyright © 2003 by Annette Cable

Published by Crown Publishers, an imprint of Random House Children's Books,
a division of Random House, Inc.,
CROWN and colophon are trademarks of Random House, Inc.

www.randomhouse.com/kids

Library of Congress Cataloging-in-Publication Data
Sweeney, Joan.
Me and my senses / by Joan Sweeney ; illustrated by Annette Cable.—1st ed.
p. cm.
Summary: Introduces the five senses using experiences from everyday life.

ISBN 0-375-81102-8 (trade)   ISBN 0-375-91102-2 (lib. bdg.)

1. Senses and sensation—Juvenile literature. [1. Senses and sensation.]
I. Cable, Annette, ill. II. Title.
QP434 .S93 2003
612.8—dc21
2002067354

Printed in the United States of America

March 2003

10 9 8 7 6 5 4 3 2 1

First Edition

This is me. Guess what I'm having for lunch?
Let's use my five senses to find out!

Ding
Dong

I hear the doorbell.
I **hear** with my ears.

I see a van out in front.
I **see** with my eyes.

This box feels warm to my touch. I **touch** with my hands.

Thank you, sir!

I smell something good. I **smell** with my nose.

"Mmmmmmm!"

PIZZA

I taste what's inside. I **taste** with my tongue.

My five senses are hearing, seeing, touching, smelling, and tasting.

Each sense works in a different way to send messages to my brain. All together they tell me the delicious news: we're having pizza for lunch!

hearing

Sound waves vibrate through my ears so I can hear.

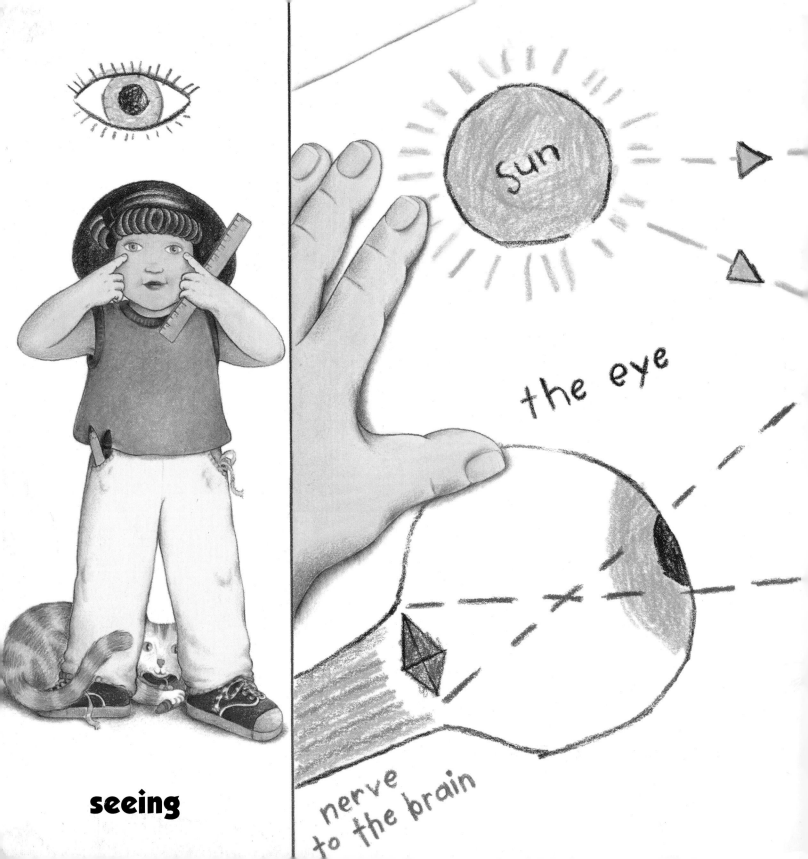

seeing

the eye

Sun

nerve to the brain

Kite

Light rays bounce off an object and send
a picture to my brain so I can see.

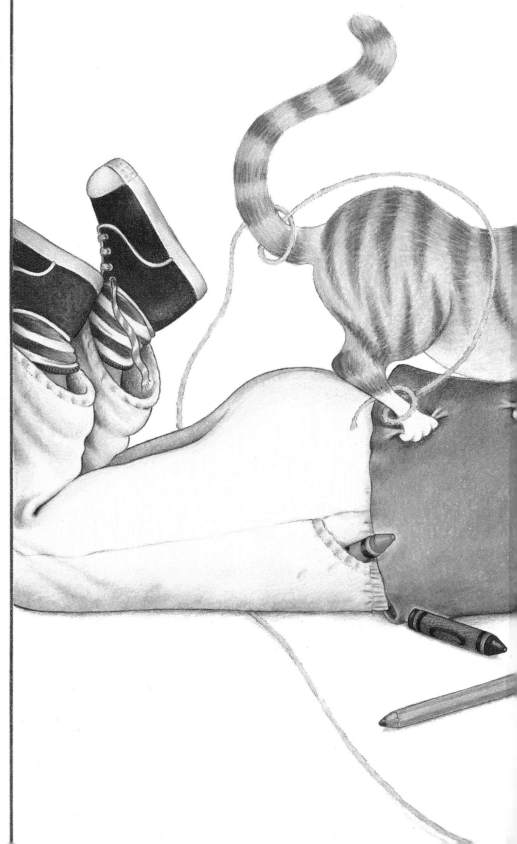

touching

Special cells in my skin tell me what's hot, cold, soft, itchy, heavy, or painful when I touch.

smelling

Over five million smell cells inside my nose tell me what's a skunk or a flower when I smell.

tasting

Tiny taste buds on my tongue tell
me if something is sweet, sour, salty,
or bitter when I taste.

Sometimes I use just one of my senses.

I hear Daddy whistle.

I smell brownies baking.

I see my book
with the help
of a flashlight.

I taste salty
crackers.

I feel cold
ice cubes.

Sometimes I use all my senses at once. I see dark clouds above while I hear thunder rumble. I feel raindrops fall and I can taste them on my tongue....

I smell the wet grass. It smells fresh and good.

Because I hear, see, touch, smell, and taste, the world makes a whole lot more sense!

Things I Can Do With My Five Senses:

 see:

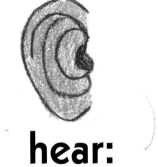 **hear:**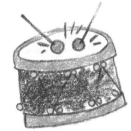

 **touch:**